entropalace

sean::adrian::brijbasi

Published simultaneously in the United
States and Great Britain in 2020
by Pretend Genius
Copyright © Sean::Adrian::Brijbasi

This book is copyright under the Berne
Convention
No reproduction without permission
All rights reserved

ISBN: 978-0-9995277-9-5

other books by Sean::Adrian::Brijbasi

One Note Symphonies
for Emma

Still Life in Motion
*for those who play
Marius and Andréus*

The Unknowed Things
for Julius

The Dictionary of Coincidences, Volume i
for Emma

S{E}AN?
for EM{M}A+

E{M}MA+ the ghost orchids
for Emma

darling two hearts
for E{M}MA+ the ghost orchids

Stories for Nadira
*for Adrian, Andréus, Elijah, Helena, Julius, Marius,
Nadira*

Play Championship World-Class
Tennis with Bjorn McEnroe
*for Adrian, Andréus, Elijah, Helena, Julius, Marius,
Nadira*

The World That Destroyed the World
for Adrian, Andréus, Elijah, Helena, Julius, Marius, Nadira

The Book of Lashonda
for Adrian, Andréus, Elijah, Helena, Julius, Marius, Nadira

for
my brother
Troy

Lelolah (lĭ-lo-la)

To live is to suffer, to survive is to find some meaning in the suffering.
--FWN

matter

outdoor blanket	1
dramatics	5
imbroglio	9
strange words to me: imbroglio	13
the good part, part i	15
the good part, part ii	19
the good part, part iii	23
the hearing of a far-seeing bird	29
anything can happen on the stairs	35
in-between-ness	41
a bicycle always looks abandoned if no one is riding it, part i	47
a bicycle always looks abandoned if no one is riding it, part ii	51
a bicycle always looks abandoned if no one is riding it, part iii	55
create your own world of being	61
strange ~~birds~~ words to me: interesting	65
a murmuration of starlings: an ode to lelolah	69
lelolah travelling with the breeze in her imagining	73
the unimportant ending of all things	77
attempting fate	81
inside my sordid body	85
entropalace	89
a permanent marker	93
list of illustrations	97

outdoor blanket

Started my day by killing a bird. Shot a sparrow with a pellet rifle from the upstairs bedroom window. Downstairs Lelolah was like what was that? Said she heard a bang and saw what looked like feathers flying out of the corner of her eye and I was like them was more than "like feathers" Lelolah, them was feathers.

She said she could still see the bird moving about in the grass and she let out some kind of bird-like screech herself that it wasn't dead yet, that the head was still moving and I said real calm, probably like one of them snipers would, "oh it's dead Lelolah, those are just them last death reflexes" and then in less than a minute the bird stopped moving to make it look like I knew what I was talking about which I did.

Lelolah wanted to go to Bartholomeu's to get an outdoor blanket and I said goddam Lelolah ain't an outdoor blanket the same as an indoor blanket except you use it outdoors and we got plenty of them. She said she didn't think they were the same—they sure didn't feel the same—but she didn't really prove it to me, just said something about different fabric, and added as a "corollary"—used the word right to my face—that we'd be nice and warm under an outdoor blanket in the fall which wasn't in no way, shape, or form, a corollary to outdoor blankets specifically but just blankets in general.

But, true to my word, I was gonna go if just to be there when the experts at Bartholomeu's tell her there ain't no such thing as outdoor blankets ma'am and they got the same fabric as indoor blankets, but I can see and hear her clear as day—already picture the scene in my head which was gonna make it more likely to happen—what she's saying about she's surprised they're not selling outdoor blankets at a fine establishment like Bartholomeu's, her parents had outdoor blankets all the time, and the person she was talking to, the man and woman who walked behind the person she was talking to, the woman working at the cash register and her boyfriend, and her boyfriend's ex-girlfriend's mama and papa, and you know she wasn't gonna forget me, would love one if we used one.

dramatics

I don't shoot birds regularly but sparrows are different. They come from Europe and before you know it start bullying all the native birds until they fly away so I decided I was gonna do a little bullying myself. I feel bad. Don't get me wrong. I always do. I get a pain in my chest for a couple minutes after I kill one but then I see the swallows and bluebirds flying around beautiful and happy and I know more sparrows are coming back anyway because there's always more of them hiding in a tree somewhere.

I'll probably feel bad about it for a good while but that's just how I'm gonna to have to feel until I steamroll that bad feeling and flatten it like nothing ever happened and the only time I'll feel it is if I flatten another bad feeling and my steamroller rolls over the spots with bad feelings it steamrolled before. I guess you'd say them spots are still tender and probably will be for all time so maybe I'm doing more camouflaging than curing.

And that's okay as long as I don't feel too bad when I'm feeling good if you know what I mean. Because sometimes when you're feeling good there's just something mixed in with it that don't make you feel quite as good as you should and something like killing a bird is one of them things.

I always promise myself that I ain't gonna kill another one but then a couple weeks later bang, feathers flying all over the place, Lelolah telling me there's gotta be another way, and me like well Lelolah if there is then tell me because killing these birds is like killing my soul which she just shrugs off with a sigh and rollin' her eyes all dramatic to mock what she says is my own dramatics: your soul? really? your goddam soul?

And I say, and I try to be serious, because killing birds is serious business, Lelolah leave my dramatics alone and then I give her that look. But secretly way deep down inside I think it ain't even dramatics. More like a feeling of being lost. Like having to rest your weary self in a strange room where everything looks clean but in the back of your mind you know is still kinda dirty and then on top of that trying to sleep on the strangest goddam pillow you ever had to lay your head on.

imbroglio

On our way to Bartholomeu's I got caught up in what you might call an imbroglio. As imbroglios go maybe it wasn't a notable imbroglio, although I'm making note of it, but it was still what any learn-ed person at a middlin' level of scholarship would call a mess.

My brother had just come down from Baltimore, gave me a call about where he was, said he could meet us at Bartholomeu's because he wanted to buy some salt and pepper shakers. Said he lost his when he was moving to his new house, loud enough through the phone for Lelolah to hear, which made her say under her breath, but knowing I could hear, something about how could any run-of-the-mill organized man lose his salt and pepper shakers which made me say, as an addendum to the conversation and loud enough for her to hear, that I'll meet you there. And I knew at that point them gears in Lelolah's brain start turning and wondering where I was talking about.

After I finished reminiscing with my brother I told her, same thing I told her before, my brother is the most organized person I know and if there was somebody more organized I ain't never met 'em my whole life so if he lost his salt and pepper shakers there was sound reason, and probably more than one, for it.

And on top of that I was gonna meet him at the bar across the road from Bartholomeu's, couldn't remember the name at the time, and have a couple drinks while she was looking for her outdoor blanket and if I get drunk in the meanwhile "captain", yeah I called her captain (not out loud, in my head), you can blame this little search party you organized for something that don't even exist, analogizin' her outdoor blanket to the whale from that book we supposed to read back in high school (again, in my head).

So I parked the car and walked in one direction, to the bar, and Lelolah walked in the other direction, to Bartholomeu's. And when I walk into the bar I see my brother and stride over to him, give him a hug—what's up boy?—order a drink, and as soon as I was about to pick my drink up to take a sip—my hand was almost touching the glass—I hear this loud bang, not like my pellet rifle, way loud, and two masked people come through the door talking about nobody move and all I could do was look at my drink which was on the bar in front of me right by my fingertips, fuckin' millimeters away, when to my horror, he or she, it was startin' to sound like a she, said everybody get on the floor and then in an instant it was like my drink was miles away and by the time I got to the floor, hundreds of miles away, because having that drink was the same thing as nothing happening and my day going on about as normal as any other day, so all I could think about was I was gonna drink it all in one fell swoop after whatever the hell was going on at the time was over and done with. But that's just what I said to the public at the time when they asked because deep down inside, again always deep deep down inside, I was only thinking about Lelolah.

strange words to me: imbroglio

Imbroglio is a word I don't use every day and if the universe synchronized itself so the words all speaking humans said at precisely the same moment were documented, the one word that would not be documented because it would not have been uttered by anyone is imbroglio.

It is both a simple and strange word which makes its definition easy on the memory, unlike other words which are complicated and strange (for example, discomfiture), their meanings forgotten should one participate in any activity that leaves one slightly breathless.

The melodious characteristics of imbroglio's structure lends itself to the opposite of its historical and current meaning—the silent g adjoining the l; the transformative marriage of the i and o subconsciously teasing an ephemeral joy or buoyancy through sound alone (the yo reflecting its fraternal twin oy).

A word that is a poem. Not for people of conviction or distributors of serious paraphernalia. A spider's dance through a field of wild poppies. Agent Aphrodite's secret code name. Or distilled to its metaphorical essence: a neatly trimmed bush with a single raspberry.

the good part, part i

Lelolah had a fine body that was filled with emotional turmoil. I tried to guess what the turmoil was a few times but only a few because you can't guess too often before people start getting mentally, emotionally, and physically tired of you.

You gotta know when to guess even if you guess right because if you guess at the wrong time, especially when you guess right, that'll leave everything teetering on the edge of an abyss staring back deep into your soul (as they say) and knowing when to guess is a guess in and of itself.

Note: when I say everything teetering, I mean everything—the past, the present, the future, the past that seems like the future, the future you can't imagine, the present that seems like the past, the present you miss because you're thinking about the past that seems like the future, and even the past you're trying to remember but can't because you're thinking about the present or as close to each side of the present as you can get. One day I guessed at the right time, but I guessed the wrong turmoil and Lelolah didn't speak to me for days (three-and-a-half).

I said: "Lelolah, this need for outdoor blankets probably represents a fear of being outside of the womb—the house or enclosed space in essence, representing the womb—and the outdoors representing the space outside of the womb, only you don't feel safe out there, like you're bare and naked in a world that's mysterious and dangerous."

I hadn't gotten to the good part of my guess yet, which described me as the delivery nurse but as a baby—like a guide—when Lelolah, without looking at me, left the room, which might make you think I was on to something but I knew in the way she didn't look at me that she wasn't angry at all. She was disappointed because I guessed wrong.

In her mind she was probably thinking I shouldn't even be guessing although she couldn't be sure I was guessing because as far as she knew, I thought I knew what I was talking about, which as it turns out, is the most right I can be about anything.

After the first hour of Lelolah not talking to me I thought if I just leave her alone then we'd be talking again in no time. After a few more hours though I thought maybe she wanted me to talk to her, but it turned out she didn't (which might have added additional hours to the "circumstance" as it wasn't a situation just yet).

After a day of her not talking to me, all I could think about was how someone could go that long without talking to someone on purpose if she didn't hate him. And then it was just hate on top of hate multiplying each day until it was all subtracted away on a Tuesday afternoon (I believe) when we saw a little girl climbing up the maple tree in our backyard (Lelolah from the bedroom window upstairs and me from the kitchen window downstairs).

the good part, part ii

I yelled out "you see that?" without even knowing Lelolah was looking out the bedroom window. "I do" she said back as if we'd been talking non-stop for days without a pause in our alliance against the forces of the world that's been battling us since the day we were born (she in the north and me in the south).

I thought "it's just you and me Lelolah" and at the same time thought to say it out loud just like that, at first in my regular voice loud enough for her to hear me upstairs and then I thought, also at the same time, maybe it would bring a more regal bearing to the circumstance if, instead, I whispered the thought loud enough for her to hear.

But it wasn't just Lelolah and me right then and there. It was Lelolah, me, and the little girl—reminding me of my eight year-old self—up in the tree and if I said out loud it's just you and me Lelolah or even whispered it then Lelolah would have said "what about that little girl?" as if I was still the barest scrap of a human being from three-and-a-half days before even though deep in the well of my conscious mind my thoughts were as pure as snowflakes falling through the air.

I was thinking about the little girl and how the three of us had become a newly formed alliance against the forces of the world that's been battling us since the day we were born and then I imagined the little girl disappearing from the tree (not literally—more like climbing up into the thicker branches and leaves of the tree so she couldn't be seen) and then appearing right next to me (literally—like the tree was a portal to whatever empty space there was to the immediate right side of my body no matter my body's state of affairs) saying in a little girl voice "you made Lelolah feel even more bare and naked in this mysterious and dangerous world" and me saying "but that's not what I was trying to do" and she saying back to me in a little girl voice with a tinge of sass "but that's what you did you dumbass".

I thought I heard a noise behind me and I turned my head, if only to distract myself from the sting of them little-girl words, but I didn't see anything and when I turned back to look through the window the little girl was gone—like she tossed an acorn behind me to make me turn my head just so she could vanish without a trace or a trail. I looked all around the tree and yard and even to my right, but I didn't see her.

When I turned around again to go upstairs Lelolah was already sitting on the seventh stair with her feet resting on the sixth and it hit me like silence being hit by the boom of an uncompromising thunder that all that time I was thinking the little girl was eight years old, she was probably no more than six and a half.

the good part, part iii

I sat on the stair next to Lelolah though there was barely enough room for the two of us and asked her how she's been doing these past three and-a-half days. She said she hadn't been sleeping and I said I know how that is Lelolah but I also know what you can do to fall asleep.

I told her I think of flowers swaying in the breeze. Roses, poppies, pansies, daisies, lilacs, and all variety of wildflowers I don't even know the names of. Sometimes the wind snaps the flowers off the stems and casts them onto a slow-moving stream, so they drift along happy in the water to beautify the world in the eyes of people who happen to catch a glimpse of them. I start thinking about flowers and I doze off as they're swaying in the field or drifting on the stream towards a horizon on the other side of which exists a land of sweet sleep and dreams we can never see from the outside as we approach ever nearer and nearer.

She said she would try in a few minutes because she was tired, and I thought so soon Lelolah? We just started talking again. But I hoped it worked for her because I didn't want her asking me any questions that might expose the *raison d'etre* of what really made me fall asleep, which wasn't flowers and which I couldn't tell her about without serious and irrevocable repercussions coming down on me that would likely lead me to a life of abandonment (from her) and exile (from the world).

I think about stabbing people I don't like. Mostly famous people but every now and then I stab a neighbor or somebody I see at the store. The conversation about her not being able to sleep caught me off guard and I wanted to say something useful since we hadn't been talking for three and-a-half days, because how would it look if the first chance I got to say something after all that time, I was silent or just uttered (what would be in her mind) nonsense? Stabbing made me think of flowers so that's what I said.

Like a rose might be a stab and a twist; a poppy a stab and then a deeper push into the already deep stab wound; amaranthus, a stab to the neck; a daffodil, a stab into the dead body of a person I've already stabbed to death in the heart, which might be a purple pansy, small and precise. And so on and so forth.

But more than the stabbing it's the warmth and smell of the blood that's a byproduct of the stabbing that makes my eyes heavy. And sometimes in my mind after I've done the stabbing or even while I'm in the throes of the stabbing I can see a big splash of blood changing the color of an antique French cushion as its being soaked up by the ancient fabric, or a tiny drop of blood landing on the white petal of a daisy that makes the petal move ever so slightly—a transference of kinetic energy in the world of nature that's almost undetectable to my human eyes.

Whatever it is, it sure makes me sleepy. But the fact of the matter is, I ain't never stabbed anybody in my life until the day we went to find an outdoor blanket at Bartholomeu's and I met my brother for a drink.

Lelolah went into the bedroom and closed the door. After a while I fell asleep on the seventh stair, just where I was sitting, and woke up five stairs later on the second stair at which point it was hardly no effort for me to just get up and walk back to the window to stare at the tree outside and think—quiet in the house and all alone (figuratively).

the hearing of a far-seeing bird

I lay with my cheek to the ground and looked at my brother who also lay with his cheek to the ground. I whispered to him that the woman brandishing that big gun and talking big almost sounds like Lelolah. He said bro that's not Lelolah, just someone who sounds like Lelolah trying to sound like a man. If she wasn't trying to sound like a man, she wouldn't sound like Lelolah at all, noting further that she probably had a high-pitched voice when she's not trying to sound like a man while Lelolah's was between high-pitched and low-pitched, almost right in the middle. Middle-pitched.

Okay, I said but what happened to your salt and pepper shakers? I can't believe you lost them when you're the most organized person I know. Don't ask he said. I could see something that looked like sadness in his eyes. Not for the lost salt and pepper shakers, in and of themselves, but from whatever story was behind the lost salt and pepper shakers. What happened man? I wanted to know so I could give Lelolah an explanation for which she would have no retort.

And then he went on to tell me this story, in a whisper, though I might have heard some parts wrong because the two people who stormed into the bar to conduct their thieving talked so goddam loud I could barely hear what he was whispering sometimes:

"I've thought for a long time there was texture missing in my life, like when you listen to a song and for whatever reason you feel like something's missing from it which makes you think scientifically and not emotionally about something being missing from your own life.

The song, and one in particular back when I was a teenager, revealed to me a hidden side, a hidden impression on the x-agon of my life that I otherwise would not have been aware of—the impression of something being missing that you can't quite put your finger on.

So, you think about the song and try to figure out what's missing. Maybe the lyrics just ain't right. Or it's missing a horn. Whatever the reason you just can't figure it out. You think you can, but you really can't because some things don't seem to grow beyond a certain point and they just are what they are, missing bits and all.

The only word I've ever thought of to describe what's missing is texture. I don't know what I mean by that, but you know what I mean right? Maybe you use another word. I don't know the first time I became aware of the impression. I might have felt it from the time I was born but just wasn't aware enough to explore it scientifically, probably due to brain development.

Maybe there ain't nothing missing but the impression I got from the song transferred itself to me and I, in essence, became that song that was missing something—horns or background singers—and I just started looking and looking for what was missing but I ain't found nothing to this day.

After a while I started thinking that maybe I'm getting an impression I shouldn't be getting. Maybe the song of my life ain't got no background singers or horns and won't grow beyond what it is. But I keep looking because I can't seem to stop and I just thought that by leaving my salt and pepper shakers behind at my old house and then lying about losing them would add some texture to my life, and a couple doo-whops or the soundscapes of a muted trumpet might emerge from the silence and fill my life with the texture I've been looking for. I tried everything else so why not?"

That's one hell of a tale I said making sure I conveyed to him with my eyes, brother to brother, that I understood what he was saying. It's okay I said, that's still better than knowing what's missing but you can't look for it. He turned his head away from me and when he did I saw a sharp knife peeking out from under his jacket, gleaming in the dusty shaft of light coming through the window.

anything can happen on the stairs

A word about the stairs in our little house. The stairs were, "if memory serves", a purgatorial transition from the every-day living area downstairs where *walking, thinking, talking, eating, sitting, sometimes reading, and further transitioning to the outside world occurred* and *the every-night living area upstairs where sleeping, thinking, talking and sometimes reading occurred.*

I never fell asleep in the downstairs area (never) and only once slept on the stairs—in the time it takes a sleeping person to transition from the seventh stair to the second stair using only his or her natural locomotive powers under sleeping conditions.

I'm a person known for my efficient and, even Lelolah can't deny, pleasing propulsion in both every-day and every-night living areas in spite of her (in my thoughts) unjustified complaints about how slowly I walked whenever we were *in flagrante delecto* and when I'd usually say something like why don't we just run Lelolah because I can run fast to which she'd reply with something like why do I even bother as she sped away from me at her normal and sometimes below average gait.

Anything can happen on the stairs though. A man can be killed, children can play chess, brothers can fight and then laugh over cold beers, but only on one stair (the eighth stair), in our little house, can you see the reflection of the old lady reading by her opened window on days when the temperature of the northern clime we reside in settles between 65 and 70 degrees Fahrenheit. Any colder or any warmer—even by the tiniest of iotas—and she's never there.

I first caught a glimpse of the old lady when I came to a full stop on the stairs one mid-day (on my descent) to pick up Lelolah's necklace and saw her reflection in the glass of the framed painting hanging on our living room wall. I paused right then and there and watched her read from her book though every once in a while she'd pick up a white tea cup and sip what I presumed and presume to this day to be tea and then hold the cup in her two hands and look out the window in a reflective pose ("a pose of reflection") as if she was lost in the thoughts inspired by the book she was reading.

There's nowhere else a person can stand, sit, or lie in our entire house—probably in the entire world, even on the roof or the back yard, adding in the vision of improved human eyesight—to see her. In fact, I challenge anyone and sometimes wish it was a real competition because I'd be the champion.

I told Lelolah about the old lady and her reflection and sometimes we'd sit on the eighth stair together and watch her read, not "like" two voyeurs but "as" two voyeurs, with a bottle of wine and delicious fruit we nibbled on like we did when we picnicked way out in the country (which was way out but not that far away).

And then one day Lelolah said "the reflection of the old lady reminds me of a dream about somebody I know but don't remember when I'm awake". I was almost asleep, half-dreaming about the leaves of a palm tree hanging over Lelolah and me and as far as I can tell there's nothing else to do with palm trees and their leaves but sit under them in silence, so maybe her words were all in my mind. I thought to myself—or I remember thinking to myself (maybe I was still in a state of half-dreaming)—that one day I'm going to knock on the old lady's door and ask her what book she's been reading and what kind of tea she's been drinking because I wanted to know more about her and I thought if I knew those two things then I'd be connected to her forever.

in-between-ness

You only have to be brave once for people to think you're a brave person. The same can be said for being a coward. You can be brave your whole life, standing up for justice, fighting the powers of evil, and then one day you waver because you're scared of getting bashed in the head or kicked in the ribs again and you become a coward in both the eyes and the hearts of the peoples of the world.

At the bar across the road from Bartholomeu's I wasn't sure what I was when I grabbed the knife I saw in my brother's jacket as we lay face down on the dusty floor. I stood up in a flash and ran toward the bandit (?), hostage-taker (?), assassin (!), but I only got half way when she turned around and pointed the cold steel "deliverer of death" (I found out later was engraved on the gun barrel) right at me, just like I had pointed mine at the sparrows in our backyard. I stopped in my tracks.

She asked me what I thought I was doing and I wanted to say "is that you Lelolah?" because it sounded so much like her but there would have been nothing stranger in the whole world—nay, the whole universe—than for Lelolah to be wearing a mask, waving a gun at people minding their own business, eating and drinking, in a bar across the road from Bartholomeu's.

And even stranger was that she was doing it with someone else and not me because, except for everyday practical matters, Lelolah and I were as difficult and troublesome to separate as a pillow and a pillow case sewn together by a master seamstress. Think of the strangest things you can think of and it wouldn't be stranger: a slippery little tadpole swimming in a cup of tea, pages of newspapers strewn about empty streets declaring an end to a war when there was no war to begin with, a box of a single crayon.

She asked me if I had something in my hand and I started to say yes but what came out of my mouth was a chirping sound. She asked if I was making fun of her and I chirped again. It was probably my fear of getting killed. I didn't know if it was a real fear, but it sure felt real, beating in my chest and my temples and perspiring all over my body. I knew the danger was real in the form of a deadly device pointed right at me, whether the person holding it wanted to kill me or not, and maybe it was normal that I couldn't control what I was saying or how I was saying it under such intense pressure. I surmised later on that it must have been all the guilt from killing those sparrows that came back on me and in my state of in-between-ness—in-between being a coward and being brave—I sounded like I was chirping.

At the time (in my desperation) I imagined birds coming from all areas (posh and unposh) of the city to help me, like a unifying army of once enemy combatants converging with a single purpose against a new and common enemy. But that was just a far-fetched dream, especially after what I had done from our bedroom window—shooting and killing without regard for bird life—and I knew in my soul that no birds were going to answer my calls for help. Not unless I changed my ways. But my ways weren't so bad, and I didn't have much to change after all. I just said to myself—I heard my voice in my thoughts normally and not like a chirping sound—"I ain't never gonna harm another bird in my life" and as quick as that I saw the shadow of a bird fly past the window of Bartholomeu's main entrance door.

a bicycle always looks abandoned if no one is riding it, part i

I read in a book I borrowed from Lelolah that some people are seen in this world of flat and far-seen places (except on the mountains and in the valleys) but really belong to a world of precipices. Precipices that appear dangerous but aren't, because along their steep downward slope a tall and soft grass grows that human hands can hold onto or the human body can nestle into if a person (who belonged to the world of precipices) fell over the side.

You might even stay there for a while and look out over the city, the city of day but mostly night, and if it had rained a recent night or if tender morning dew had collected on the tufted incline, the cool and sweet-smelling water could sustain you, if you wanted to linger there for such a time, even on the steamiest days (and on the most reckless days that felt like nights) as long as your mind was at peace because you knew that your bicycle, which threw you in an act of love as you tried to navigate the curve too fast (again), was undisturbed and safe from the ravages of time or from tempted passers-by (because a bicycle always looks abandoned if no one is riding it).

You might even fall asleep, nestling your head on the softest patch of nature's cozy pillow, while night, in its way, the most detached of voyeurs, watches over you—though without regard for your well-being or the well-being of your bicycle. There might even be other humans around you, who do not belong to the world of precipices, and who had tumbled like a ball rolling from the playground asphalt into the high grass, unseen by others who had also tumbled, lost and waiting to be rescued, like a ball is rescued from the high grass by the hand of a child.

But as soon as you heard any creaking sound, a sound which gave you a feeling of dread because you heard all your life about the crushing effects of nature's raw atmosphere on the frames of bicycles (something you didn't want to see with your own eyes)—maybe a bird crying out like the exposed metal at the bottom of a wooden gate scraping the sidewalk—you would start your climb back to the top, though careful not to pull any grass from the earth as you made your ascent.

a bicycle always looks abandoned if no one is riding it, part ii

I saw the little girl who had climbed the tree in our backyard talking to the old lady at her front door whose house I was riding by on my bicycle to see if she might be out tending to her flowers so I could talk to her, maybe ask her what I always wanted to ask her, i.e. what book she's been reading lately. I was carrying the book Lelolah let me borrow so that if I did see the old lady, she would be instantly drawn to the person (unknown to her—me) carrying a book and perhaps strike up a conversation with him (me) about his (my) book, books in general, and the book she was reading at the time.

I thought here I go again, the dissonant note of a tritone (the devil's interval) like I've been at least four (4) times in the recent past:

1. Lelolah, me, and the little girl;

2. my brother, me, and the woman bandit;

3. the stairs, me, and Lelolah;

4. Lelolah, me, and outdoor blankets; and now

5. the little girl, me, and the old lady.

My plan was to dismount from my bicycle and walk it past the old lady's house as I pretended to read, or really read, from my book—maybe whisper some sentences out loud to create a moment of magic in the old lady's eyes, but a moment that lasted in her memory, as she saw me walk by—something to match the birds flying around her yard: *"there is a relationship between music and flying that has yet to be studied. For example, how the arc of a crow's flight influences the texture of a Beethoven sonata. Or how the delicate shifts of a pigeon's wing affect cadence in a Mahler symphony or a Janacek concerto*".

But when I saw the old lady standing on her stoop talking to the little girl I panicked and forgot to dismount from my bicycle. My plan had gone awry in a flash. Or so I thought. But it had been doomed from the start as the old lady and the little girl probably had a plan to meet for a while that, unknown to me all that time, neutralized my own plan before it was ever put into action. And though I was known by everyone (I knew) as someone who panicked quickly, I was equally known for thinking quickly after I panicked, which Lelolah said was an enviable quality itself and nothing to laugh at.

I dropped the book right in front of the old lady's house and kept on riding. I didn't look back until I was further down the road when I stopped and watched her walk past the little girl (like she wasn't there) to pick up the book, possibly forgetting the little girl's name and face or that she even existed, in the few seconds it took to do so. I knew in that moment that if the old lady could forsake the little girl standing right there in front of her, to pick up a book that was a stranger to her, then I'd be able to stop by her house, ask her for my book, and talk to her in a way that made her think I was saying interesting things about my book, books in general, and the particulars of the life around us.

a bicycle always looks abandoned if no one is riding it, part iii

I didn't sleep the whole night before the day I was going to ride to the old lady's house and knock on her door and ask her for my book that I dropped the day before as a ruse to then ask her what book she's been reading lately and to have a conversation with her about my book, books in general, and the particulars of the life around us.

I lay in bed with Lelolah already sleeping beside me, while thoughts appeared and disappeared in my mind like they were photographs added and removed by the beak of the hungriest woodpecker in the forest, and furthermore like they were appearing and disappearing at the same time, at the speed of the bird's true-to-life pecking frenzy.

In that state of mind I couldn't sleep and thought about getting up, silently walking to the stairs ("like a cat"), and sitting down on the eighth stair to look at the glass of the framed painting in which I had seen the reflection of the old lady reading in her window so many times.

But Lelolah turned towards me and though she was still in the depths of her sleep it seemed as if she was looking at me from behind her closed eyelids, watching me, thinking unconscious and semi-unconscious thoughts about the foolishness of my nervous behavior while she (at the same time) dreamt about our happy days together. I watched her with my open eyes and soon drifted into a half-sleep in which I half-dreamt about the leaves of a palm tree swaying over us as a light breeze gamboled on the hairs of our brows and lashes—the same half-dream I've been having since the day we first met.

The next day I waited until afternoon to ride my bicycle to the old lady's house. I told Lelolah I had to buy a new pedal from the store, which was true, but what she didn't know—which was even more true—was that the biggest part of my day's adventure was going to happen on the way there. I tried not to ride faster than usual but I could tell my speed was above average and I pushed my bicycle's velocity to its limits, so by the time I arrived at the old lady's house my legs were more tired than they've ever been. And though my calf and thigh muscles ached, and I was breathless for a minute, I was happy when I saw my book on the stoop by the front door.

I parked my bicycle on the sidewalk (using the formal kickstand), and as I walked toward the book, I saw the old lady through the window moving around in her house. The book itself looked more beautiful than ever (though I never thought to describe it in such a way) and it was clear to me the old lady had done something (cleaned it or decorated it or maybe did something beguiling to it) to make it look so good.

I rang the doorbell, but she didn't answer. I knocked on the door a couple times but still no answer. Then I heard a tapping on the window and looked over and saw her waving from inside, like she was waving good-bye, even though she had yet to wave hello—a good-bye wave which froze me in my place. She disappeared further into her house and I stood there for a few seconds, unsure of what to do, waiting to hear the door unlock, but she didn't come back.

I rode home, disappointed but not sad, because I could always stop disappointment from becoming sadness by thinking about worst things that could have happened. I went upstairs and lay in bed. It was afternoon, middle afternoon, and I was feeling sleepy, and it would be the first time I fell asleep in the afternoon since I was a baby—the first time I became aware that falling asleep in the afternoon, like an old lady might fall asleep, made me see faces of people from my past whose names I couldn't remember, and who existed only in a world that I saw as my mind moved towards sleep, like when you'd see the sparsely populated landscape and the fleeting faces of the people who lived there, through the window of a moving train.

create your own world of being

The woman bandit and I were like two children who didn't belong to one place or the other and who clung to each other in a world that was strange to us because of the imbalance caused by us thinking we belonged here (wherever here was) but no one else thinking the same. The no-one's who were sometimes polite but who nonetheless never would or could (out of fear or laziness) just let us be. But in the end, we were fearful and lazy too, and agreed we didn't belong here either, because we didn't want to belong to a place where such an imbalance was allowed and mostly encouraged—an imbalance that's been compound-multiplying since the beginning of time, and that our little human bodies, no matter the size, were too light to tip one way or the other on any measurable scale. That was our secret even as we outwardly fought to bring balance to the world we were forced by birth or circumstance to live in because we had no choice.

I felt as I stood there in front of her that we were just one lingering conversation away from starting over as friends and that if I could find the right conversation to have with her then everybody would be safe and maybe she (and the man bandit) would leave as if nothing happened. I wanted them to leave as if nothing happened because I knew only the most desperate people (desperados) would storm into a place where people were loitering peacefully and threaten their lives. I suppose they could have been evil too but I didn't sense any evil emanating from them.

I said I understand what you're doing lady bandit (I called her lady even though in my mind I was thinking "woman"). I understand you're trying to tip the scales of imbalance and bring some balance to the world because you mostly can't just be and when you're being, something or somebody just won't let you be. But you know like I know that ain't never gonna happen and this is just where we living right now. We gotta be in this world of people that mostly won't let us be. And the ones who do let us be, don't really want to until we're gone. That's a secret in their hearts they won't never confess to. All their talk and proclamations lady bandit about humankind are just like the dainty chirpings of a songbird, chirping out a *petite belle* song that don't last but a few seconds and disappears faster into the ether than a diving peregrine falcon, the world's fastest creature.

At the end of my soliloquy I made whistling sounds like the chirpings of a night bird, and then I went dramatically silent. You could hear a few people in Bartholomeu's breathing it was so silent. The woman bandit walked over to me (the sound of her footsteps mysteriously in-tune with the silence) without taking her eyes off me, got right up to my face, and told me to get back down on the floor or she was gonna knock me out with the butt of her gun—something she said she didn't want to do but would do if I gave her no choice. I started sensing a little evil in that moment and went back to where my brother was and lay down on my stomach right next to him. The woman bandit kept looking at me and then she whistled (also like a night bird) for a few seconds before the room fell silent again, and I heard what she was saying.

strange ~~birds~~ words to me: interesting

Unlike the strange word "imbroglio", the strange word "interesting" is a word I use every day. It wouldn't be out of place in any of my life settings for me to say without any observable prompting: "interesting".

When I'm walking by myself and I see something I can't make sense of or if I'm sitting down with somebody and talking to them and they say something I don't understand now and probably never will understand. It's the word for what my mind is feeling when a "something-to-be-understood-that-others-understand" is as vague to me as an impenetrable fog in which my ears hear the caw-caw-cawing of common ravens (corvus corax—smartest of all birds) but my eyes—because of my singular mind—only see the suggestion of common ravens flying to and fro as shadowy figures in the grey muddle.

The word comes from two sound fractions (inter = in-between and esse = to be) and when you add those two sound fractions together you get another whole sound fraction that means something like: *in between being*—which approaches the parabolic curve of my general bewilderment in the way a dripping, wet sock fits a dry foot—tight and snug but unpleasant.

If "imbroglio" is a single raspberry on a neatly-trimmed bush, then "interesting" is a raspberry bush in the late summer after the leaves have fallen off and then into fall and winter when it's just sticks before it's pruned down, and then again in spring when the new shoots start growing.

All of those different times in the seasons, in between being a seed and the leafless canes of winter, states of 1) becoming a raspberry bush and 2) being a raspberry bush, without 3) being the raspberry bush—green, lush, and full of red raspberries—the way my eyes (because of my singular mind) like to see it.

a murmuration of starlings: an ode to lelolah

Lelolah said she's been seeing things more clearly than ever and by things she's not talking about ideas or feelings, she's talking about actual things—objects in the world, especially the ones with color and I said they all have color Lelolah but she said even the ones with just a little color, the more grey objects and she said she can't explain why but she thinks it's because all of a sudden her eyesight's been going bad, and she thinks she's going blind, even though she's still young and beautiful (two words bound together by reflections of erstwhile times), so when she's looking at something, she says she's looking at it like it's the last time she'll see it because she's going to wake up the very next morning and be blind, so that what looks like a single color green to me looks like every kind of color green to her—for example, in a blade of grass she might see lime green, avocado green, dark sea green, jungle green—seeping in and out of each other, and the same for all the other colors on whatever object she's staring at, and I asked her wouldn't it be better to see faces more clearly Lelolah because suppose you forget what people's faces look like, especially mine, and she said it's okay if she forgets people's faces because she'll never forget mine, even in all the blindness that's going to inhabit her world for the rest of her days, but if she forgets the colors, she feels like she'll be lost and everything in her mind will be blind with blind outlines, meaning she won't be able to imagine things as separate so if I, for example, lead her by her hand outside on a cool, fall day and say Lelolah there's a murmuration of starlings dappling the blue sky, for her it'll just be blindness, like the greens seeping into each other but instead of greens it'll be blindness seeping into blindness, and the words themselves won't make any sense, and imagining a murmuration of starlings in her mind's eye will be the same as imagining the blue sky or a pencil or a foot, and I said Lelolah you're way too smart for me, always have been, and I'll never understand what you're talking about (sometimes) but it don't matter if you go blind or forget what my face looks like because I'll love you until the day I die and she said that's all you ever say when you don't understand what I'm talking about but she smiled when she was saying it.

lelolah travelling with the breeze in her imagining

I didn't know what was going on at Bartholomeu's while my brother and I were held hostage in the bar across the road. For all I knew there might have been a coordinated attack across the city (bandits here, bandits there, bandits every-etc.) and Lelolah might have been on the floor of the linen aisle—a hostage herself—holding onto an outdoor blanket she had picked out to buy.

It wouldn't have surprised me if not long after she was ordered to get down on the floor that she took advantage of the time to cast a more critical eye at the outdoor blanket as she lay still—unwrapped it (illegally) from its package and felt its texture on the tenderest part of her cheek, or covered her sandaled but un-socked foot with a corner of the moderately thick but soft fabric just to see how much warmth it would provide on a cooler-than-expected, late-summer night as all variety of bird life migrated across the dark skies above us.

She was always good at imagining the weather. She could imagine it being blazing hot in the middle of winter and start sweating right before my eyes. Or she could imagine a cold, arctic blast of wind moving through our backyard paradise on the hottest day of summer so that when she pressed her body against mine to get warm, her skin felt like the outside of an ice bucket filled with melting ice cubes, which always feels good when the sun is at its most intense in the space around you and the sun rays are burning you up.

My favorite of her imaginings of the weather though is when she's imagining a warm, breezy day and she closes her eyes and starts breathing so I can hear her breath—sighs flowing in and out of her elegant lungs—like the incoming and outgoing tides of the vast ocean whispering in both my ears at the same time.

She said that when she's imagining a warm, breezy day with her eyes closed she's also imagining her mother running along the beach as a little girl though she can't get the imagining quite right since she's never seen any photographs of her mother's face when she was a little girl because, as her mother said to her one afternoon when they were drinking tea on the front porch and talking about old times: "nobody had a camera back then".

So she'd imagine the breeze itself moving over the sand and the rocks towards a road that runs perpendicular to the beach and to a house, up through a back window of the house, to a small room, where a little girl slept on a small bed inside a mosquito net, but turned on her side—away from the window and the light—so that the breeze (and Lelolah travelling with the breeze in her imagining) moved through the net and over the small bed and the surface of the girl's little body to reach her face but (alas) never to see it.

the unimportant ending of all things

Lelolah said she's been in situations where things ended badly and I said me too Lelolah and she said she didn't want things to end badly between us and I said why do things have to end at all when there's no end in sight and she said the end has to be in sight, whether you see it or not, you should know the end is always there, on the verge of happening, and be prepared for it in the depths of your hidden mind so when it happens there won't be any shame in the ending which made me think about my past endings and I realized she was right about all of them, that I couldn't remember them without feeling an element of shame in each of them, like argon or magnesium, unseen and deniable but undoubtedly there—either due to my inexperience or indifference or worst of all my cruelty with a place, a situation, or a person—so that when it comes to our end she said we should end with the right amount of elegance and kindness so we remember the end as fondly as we remember the beginning and everything that happened in between, so that the end is as important as the beginning and everything that happened in between, meaning the end is no more or no less important than the beginning and everything that happened in between and therefore, she said "the inescapable logic follows" (her words) unimportant, but I questioned her logic out loud "don't seem inescapable to me" (my words) and she retorted that some logics aren't about being inescapable they're just about being and how you want to live in this sad world we're stitched into so tight and I said "that makes sense to me Lelolah" but my head started hurting when I tried to think about what she was saying because it was yet one more thing she talked about that I didn't understand and no matter how hard I tried, my hidden mind kept reaching its limit, and I couldn't understand anymore, like when I think about the universe and its vast scale and the cold darkness of endless space.

attempting fate

I was back on the floor lying next to my brother when the thought occurred to me that maybe I could attempt fate by doing something so out of the ordinary that the lady bandit would think something peculiar was wrong with me and decide to end her siege once and for all so people of all ages in the bar (no one under 18) could go back to their normal lives, including her.

No one could see what she looked like behind her mask, although I thought the improvised machinations of her voice and the unusual vocal range of just what I would call everyday human-to-human dialogue, gave some of her more subtle features away. I would never reveal my thoughts about her subtle features to anyone though, because she and I shared a moment of understanding (beyond the understanding of people not letting us be) that made me vow in my mind I would never give voice, neither in spoken word nor song, about any of her subtle features (or what I perceived them to be), even the perceived color of one strand of hair on her head that might have been this color or that color as she moved into and out of the different spectra of light illuminating the dusky spaces of the room.

I wanted her to get away clean—like she was Lelolah and I was her partner—but more than that I wanted to leave a lasting impression in her mind and the mind of the man bandit of what happened there and what I did—how reckless I was indeed in the face of danger (although I had failed once)—so that when they looked back on the event from a safe location they would say to themselves and maybe to each other that what happened was meant to be—it was fate—and couldn't have ended any other way even though it probably could have ended a hundred different ways and maybe more than that. That's why attempting fate is so powerful.

But before I could do anything, as I was still planning in my mind, my brother stood up and looked at the lady bandit, although I couldn't tell if he made eye contact with her, then he turned around and picked up his drink from the bar and drank it down in one fell swoop (I could hear his drinking style) like I had planned on doing after this was all over.

The lady bandit started walking over to him but before she could take a third step I stood up and turned around next to my brother and drank my drink in one fell swoop and slammed my glass on the lacquered mahogany with more conviction than I had ever slammed a glass on lacquered mahogany before.

My brother and I looked at each other in the mirror that decorated the wall behind the bar. The last thing I remember, although I found out afterwards that more things happened, was me thinking: there we were, two brothers attempting fate, two brothers living our lives during an event of unusual unpredictability layered on top of the usual unpredictability of events that have come to guide our everyday living like a stream that's dug a groove in this hard earth and carries along whatever small objects have fallen into it.

inside my sordid body

I confess to all the world that it was only after I met Lelolah that I started living what you might call an extrasomatic existence whereas before I was just living inside my sordid body, relying on the rudimentary functions within to keep me moving from one place to the next, one day to the next.

Then I met Lelolah and my existence changed. She gave me books to read, she taught me how to read her way (she said), and told me that I had to "awaken my soul" to the subtle and indescribable beauty of the world sidling beside me in the blind-spots of my existence—in the same way I might have to open my ears to catch the melody of a barely-perceptible song emanating from another room.

She said she didn't want to live on this earth for such a short while with anyone whose soul wasn't awakened at all times, so if I wanted to be on this earth with her then I had to find a way to awaken mine. She proposed that I start with flowers because they're one of the most beautiful things in nature but that didn't work because they didn't move around unless they were swaying in the breeze, and at the time, I was all about action—running fast, improvising animated gestures, punching out in the air.

If I wanted action she said, maybe I should try birds. It was my last chance (as she waved good-bye to me at the bus stop—don't go Lelolah), and so I started watching birds—birds of different shapes and colors, different sounds and flying patterns, different ways of pecking at the grass, landing, walking, taking off—which, without me realizing it, and only after a few weeks, did awaken my soul to the subtle and indescribable beauty of the world, and so much so that the next time I saw Lelolah I didn't even have to tell her my soul was awakened. She just knew, because even if having an awakened soul was something people could hide, it wasn't something they could lie about, especially (quote-unquote) someone with eyes like yours.

She said my soul was probably waking up before I even met her and for one reason or another it kept going back to sleep before it lifted itself up from the bed and she just happened to pass by at the right time to give it that one last little lift—barely a pinky lift—to get itself up and going. But awakening my soul to the beauty of the world also made me more perturbed and easily agitated, first by birds that didn't allow the beauty of other birds to take wing (therefore the wave of shooting and killing), and then by people, who heard only what was loud and saw only what was obvious.

entropalace

It's only when you're near the end that you can see the end. At least that's the case in my case. Everything that happens builds toward an ending but sometimes before an ending comes into relief I see a sketch of it—days, weeks, months, or years before, depending on what is ending—because after some time the end of a thing starts to take shape, gets colored in, the form of it presses against the mechanism I use for everyday living, sometimes changing it, sometimes rerouting circuitry so the electricity that once fired through it in all directions and gave it life no longer does or dissipates at a terminal no longer connected to the whole of my living.

Bodies once attached to places on a map or dates on a calendar become detached and float above me and all the neglected monuments of our common history. Questions I ask every day and for which I await answers are no longer asked. For example, how did this happen? And why, over the billions of years the universe has been calculated to have existed, did everything lead to this?

And though I had stopped asking I was still hoping answers would present themselves to me while I was doing other things, and in fact, answers did present themselves to me when I was in the bar with my brother while Lelolah was in the shop across the road searching for an outdoor blanket that she and I would warm ourselves under during colder nights by (or not by) a fire, but I was in a dream-like state underneath a palm tree (on the floor, beneath the bar stool, after I was knocked out cold by the lady bandit—something she said she would do that she didn't want to do but that she did) while my brother battled her and the man bandit single-handedly, subduing them both until help arrived.

When I finally woke up later that day I didn't remember the words in the answers that presented themselves to me but I did remember my brother and I looking at each other on the floor, the lady bandit standing in the doorway, the man bandit standing next to her, the spectra of light in the room, a breeze coming from the ocean, the sound of a drinking glass banging against a table, the shadow of a bird passing by the window, a bicycle fallen on its side, an old lady sitting by a window reading a book, a little girl climbing a tree, the color green, a necklace gleaming on the stairs in our house, the name of the bar, and Lelolah smiling at me.

a permanent marker

Weeks passed after Lelolah bought her outdoor blanket at Bartholomeu's, but she had yet to take it out of its see-through plastic package. She put it away in our bedroom closet because the nights outside had become too warm since her impulse to buy one and she didn't want to imagine cold nights and cover herself with it while I sat across from her or beside her, uncovered.

Then one cooler night when I went outside, I saw the outdoor blanket under the light of a waning gibbous moon (my second favorite), unfolded, and laid out across the grass on the edge of our patio. It (the outdoor blanket) was decorated with images of different birds—a song sparrow, a cardinal, a red-winged blackbird, etc.—and I looked to see if I recognized them all, which I did, and

I thought that if recognizing birds decorating an outdoor blanket was a real competition then I'd be the champion because I recognized every one of them in record time and if I had to do it again I would recognize them even faster.

I leaned down and touched the fabric of the outdoor blanket, moved my hand across the images of the birds, and thought Lelolah was right all along because the outdoor blanket felt so different to my fingertips than any indoor blanket I had ever touched.

A few minutes later Lelolah came outside and sat down on our patio loveseat and asked me to bring the outdoor blanket over so she and I could "cover ourselves beneath it and feel the temperature of our bodies transform slowly to a temperature that would be the best temperature our bodies would ever feel in our whole lives as the outdoor blanket synchronized our journey to the perfect degrees of a shared bliss".

We were on our way to those perfect degrees too—I could feel it all over my skin—when I noticed the images of the birds on the outdoor blanket were missing their eyes, and I said to Lelolah these birds are missing their eyes, and she said to me it was the last outdoor blanket at the shop and she told them the same thing so they gave her a discount and (continuing on before I could ask her how much) said she knew I'd realize the eyes were missing sooner or later but if I didn't, she was going to tell me after giving me enough time to make the observation myself.

She moved her hand from beneath the outdoor blanket and gave me a black felt tip pen (a permanent marker) and said we could color the eyes in ourselves.

--end--

list of illustrations

1. *Archilochus colubris*
2. *Sialia sialis*
3. *Thryothorus ludovicianus*
4. *Corvus brachyrhynchos*
5. *Cyanocitta cristata*
6. *Zenaida macroura*
7. *Dryocopus pileatus*
8. *Tachycineta bicolor*
9. *Sturnus vulgaris*
10. *Cardinalis cardinalis*
11. *Sitta carolinensis*
12. *Spinus tristis*

www.ingramcontent.com/pod-product-compliance
Lightning Source LLC
Chambersburg PA
CBHW030907170426
43193CB00009BA/769